Gütermann
Thread Painting

by Liz Hubbard

SEARCH PRESS

Introduction

Front cover and previous page:

Nasturtium sewing box.
*Dimensions 12in. wide × 10½in.
deep and 5in. high
(30cm. × 13.75cm. × 12.5cm.).*

*The Nasturtium picture which is set
in the lid of the sewing box is a
straightforward 'Thread Painting'.
I chose the theme for its startling
colours and 'satiny' leaves. The
sewing is confined to the area of the
flowers and leaves, with the top left
background remaining unstitched.*

*The box itself was one I made
from pieces of card, to fit the picture;
but a ready-made box could be
adapted and a special picture done
in the appropriate proportions.*

*A hole was cut in the lid, the right
size for the picture. I then covered
the top with a dupion furnishing
fabric, before inserting the 'Thread
Painting' and glueing it into place.
A lining was made to cover the
underside of the lid, and disguise
the back of the picture.*

*I covered and lined the bottom
half of the box in a similar way using
dupion, dress lining and latex glue.
In this instance, the box was large
enough for me to make a lift-out tray
with lined compartments, to carry
thread, scissors, etc.*

'Thread Painting' is an innovatory art form, using the exciting range of colours now available in Gütermann polyester dressmaking thread, and an electric sewing machine as the tool with which to apply them.

It is a development of free-style machine embroidery and belongs to the category of needlecrafts which offers considerable scope for creativity. If taken to its fullest potential, it can be said to bridge the gap between crafts and fine art.

The visual effects of 'Thread Painting' are quite remarkable. Images take shape quickly and strongly and retain their initial vitality. It can best be regarded as an absorbing new picture-making medium, which has special qualities of colour intensity, and texture. Pictures made by this method often look like an oil painting, having the additional fascination of a stitched surface, which becomes apparent on closer inspection.

As soon as the work begins, pictures start to take on characteristic depth and richness which seem to bring the scene to life. Colours retain a particular vibrance because the threads mingle but do not merge with one another. Light plays on the direction and texture of the stitches, giving the surface the quality of deliberate brush marks.

It is a stimulating technique to use. The images can grow at almost the speed of thinking out the next step. There are no special stitches to learn, and very few do's and don'ts to remember.

'Thread Painting' begins with the selection of a piece of fabric. This is stretched tight on an embroidery hoop. The design or picture is painted on roughly, as a guide for the stitching, and in order to soften the background.

The actual stitches which a sewing machine makes are similar to the zigzag marks made by a child when crayonning. 'Thread Painting' utilises this characteristic. The machine becomes a drawing tool, with the picture able to move freely underneath the needle in any direction, to achieve the lines and patches of colour.

As will naturally happen in a new painting medium, the individual will develop his or her own artistic style.

Broads Landscape

Broads landscape painting

The little watercolour sketch of a Norfolk Broads landscape was the basis for the 'Refracted Image'.

Following page:

Refracted image. *Framed size 14in. × 12in. (35cm. × 30cm.); image area 9in. × 7in. (22.5cm. × 17.5cm.).*

The little watercolour sketch of a Norfolk landscape.featured colours and shapes that I wished to develop into a more abstract painting. By re-drawing and tracing these simplified stages on to the calico, and using only a few of the original colours to paint the background, I managed to lose some of the 'photographic' qualities of the original.

I superimposed an abstract rectangle on to the image with the intention of causing a shift of textures like that of a view through bevelled glass. When I began stitching, I found it necessary to use direction of the threads more positively than usual, to compensate for the limited colour range, and in order to emphasise the 'refraction' that I had hoped to achieve within the boundaries of the rectangle.

The finished image has a surrealist quality far removed from the original scene.

Bluebells (painted calico)
The painted calico stage of 'Bluebells in woodland' clearly demonstrates that you only need a sketchy painting as your theme and guide.

Previous page:

Abstract with flowers. *Framed size 10in. × 10in. (25cm. × 25cm.); image area 6¾in. × 6¾in. (approx. 17cm. × 17cm.).*

This little picture was painted with blobs and splashes of dusky greens, blues and purples. The only part which shows a drawing is the half hidden flower pedestal.

It is an example of the easiest kind of 'Thread Painting', and is a good subject for a beginner to choose. There is no difficult drawing or painting involved, and any mistakes can be easily hidden.

I simply picked out areas in the painted stage, and embellished them with a suitable colour and texture. The flower pedestal is emphasised in dark straight stitch to give the picture something solid to attract the eye, but a beginner would not need to include this.

The flowers are only blobs of bright colour, some with tiny yellow centres. I have included some leaf shapes in the foreground, made by widening and narrowing the stitch width.

Bluebells (semi-stitched)
'Bluebells in woodland' in its semi-stitched stage, to show how splashes and blobs of colour begin to take shape once you start to stitch the painting.

Following page:

Bluebells in woodland. *Framed size 16in. × 16in. (40cm. × 40cm.); image area 10½in. × 10½in. (26.25cm. × 26.25cm.)*

As with most of my paintings, I started working on the part farthest away from the onlooker. In this case, I began with some very light greens for sunlit trees beyond the crown of the hilly path. I then applied some tree trunks and branches on top of these, and so on, until I had reached the detail in the foreground.

On the right-hand side I stitched in some fern shapes with a tiny zigzag, and also some more clearly defined bluebell spikes near the bottom of the circle.

Materials and equipment

Previous page:

Bluebells in woodland. *Bluebell woods can be expressed in a fresh and lively way by the medium of 'Thread Painting'.*

This picture has been followed stage-by-stage in photographs showing how it develops. The enlargement of a small area demonstrates just how random the stitches are in reality. They work like brush marks in an oil painting, having the desired visual effect at a normal viewing distance.

As some or most of the materials you will need can already be found in the home, a start can be made without too much expense. The following list will help the beginner to gather together the essentials for 'Thread Painting'.

1. Fabric for the background
Use any firm, closely woven material; but bear in mind that you will cover it in places with stitches that will distort and pull the fabric. (A heavy, unbleached calico is recommended. It is akin to artists' canvas).

2. Paints or dyes
Any quick-drying artists' paints, such as watercolours or acrylics, are the most suitable.

There are some excellent fabric paints and dyes now available, specifically developed for printing or spraying on to cloth. Be careful to choose dyes and background fabrics which are compatible, according to the instructions on the dye stuff packets.

3. Thread
You will need a good quality sewing thread that does not knot and is available in an extensive range of colours. Gütermann Sew-All thread is ideal for this new technique by virtue of its extensive colour range, its fineness combined with strength, and its knot-free quality. Made from 100% polyester, it will not fade and is resistant to mildew and abrasion.

Standard polyester dressmaking threads can also be used for 'Thread

The essentials for 'Thread Painting' are: calico, 12in. embroidery hoop, paints, dyes, brushes and a good selection of Gütermann sewing threads.

Painting'. They are also resistant to fading in daylight, and to damage from atmospheric pollution.

If you already have a few colours in part used spools, these could form the basis upon which to build your own collection of threads.

4. Wooden embroidery hoop

Choose a simple hoop, ensuring that it will slip under the head of your sewing machine. To begin with, at least, it is good to be able to see the whole of your work at once; so, ideally, the hoop will be large enough to enclose the full size of your 'Thread Painting'. The largest hoop available is 12 inches (30 centimetres) diameter, but for a first piece of work a smaller size will probably be more suitable.

5. Domestic sewing machine

Most of the familiar makes of electric sewing machine can be used for this technique. It is important that the feed teeth (which move the fabric under the presser foot in normal seam sewing) can be lowered, or covered up with a special plate. This enables the work to move about freely under the needle.

It is desirable to have zigzag facilities, but it is not necessary to have a machine which incorporates sophisticated patterns.

6. Additional items

You will also need pencils, brushes and small scissors for the picture-making. Also needle and thread, and a piece of strong card for stretching the work when it is finished.

Following page:

Halvergate marshland. *Framed size 16in. × 16in. (40cm. × 40cm.); image area 10½in. × 10½in. (26.25cm. × 26.25cm.).*

The composition of this painting is very simple. The top half is almost all sky, only broken by an interesting tree line. The lower half is nearly all grassland, giving me an excuse to blend colours together to give a wild undulating, effect.

These Norfolk reed marshes change throughout the year. Here I have captured a brief moment when the green sedges are putting up flower heads, and the whole landscape is tinged with warm pinky browns.

Once again I have added a little leafy and grassy detail at the front, just to confirm to the eye that the scene has depth and distance.

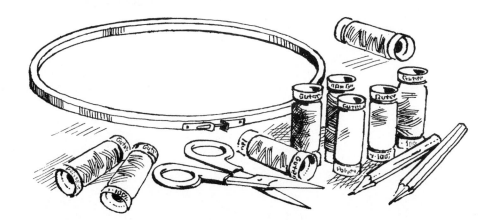

Method

Previous page:

Autumn lane. *Framed size 14in. × 12in. (40cm. × 35cm.); image area 9in. × 7in. (22.5cm. × 17.5cm.).*

During the time that I have spent developing my 'Thread Painting' technique, I have become increasingly interested in the use of colour in light or shade.

'Autumn lane' is quite a simple picture. The autumn trees, just beginning to take on that burnt bright colour, were intensified by the low angle of the sun, and the striking shadows across the road.

I have not exaggerated the pinks and oranges, or the purply blue of the shadows.

'Thread Painting' is a fluid technique. The 'feel' of free embroidery is strange to the beginner, who may be used to a degree of directional pull in normal, feed-assisted sewing. With the feed dog lowered or covered up, according to the make of sewing machine, there is no automatic control of stitch length or direction. Both will now depend upon manual movement of the embroidery hoop.

A little practice is a good idea. After reading the following description of method, try doodling on a spare piece of fabric in the hoop, in order to develop your manoeuvering skills. The exercise could be treated similarly to the testing of a new pen or brush to see what marks you can make with it.

Try writing your name. It could be useful later for signing your pictures!

Stage 1. Putting the fabric into the hoop

The background fabric needs to be stretched taut in the embroidery frame. If the fabric is likely to slip loose, you may need to bind the inner ring with tape or bias binding, to give extra grip.

1. Iron out any creases in the fabric.
2. Place outer ring on a table.
3. Lay fabric over outer ring, right side up (see Fig. 1).

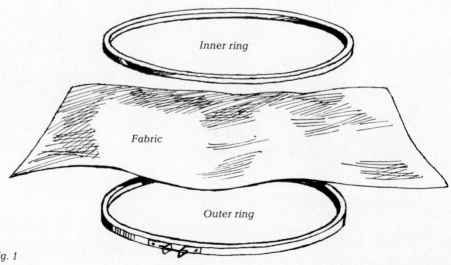

Fig. 1

4. Slip inner ring over fabric, and press down into the larger outer ring. Tighten hoop, keeping the weave as straight as possible. Your work should now be right way up to paint on, with the fabric flat on the table top and the edges of the hoop standing up around the fabric (see Fig. 2).

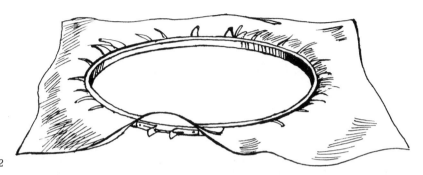

Fig. 2

Stage 2. Painting the design

This stage is the beginning of the picture-making. It has two purposes.

First, it transforms a blank piece of cloth into a 'blueprint' for the stitches, and will dictate to some extent how the pictures will develop.

Second, it has the advantage of softening the background, and eliminating the need to cover up every part of the surface with stitches. It is a good idea to leave some areas of paint showing. For instance, sky and stone might not look natural if filled in. In an abstract work, areas of paint give some rest to the eye, in contrast to heavily encrusted texture.

Painting on to material is an enjoyable process. The colour does not flow as it can on paper. If you require a washy effect, damp the fabric first, and then apply paint, which will run and blend. If you want a crisp line or edge, then dry any existing wet patches (with a hairdryer for speed) and paint again on top.

For other effects one could try spraying or dabbing with a sponge.

It is worth remembering that painting is used largely as a basis for embellishment with threads, so it is unnecessary to overwork this stage, unless you have decided to leave certain sections unstitched. These areas may need to show some refinement of paintwork.

Your first picture need not be a very complicated one. If you have not painted pictures before, try doodling on paper, or make an 'ink blot' pattern. Splashes of your favourite colours could be turned into an exciting abstract work; or might be picked out to look like bunches of

Previous page:

Copse in winter. *Framed size 16in. × 14in. (40cm. × 35cm.); image area 9in. × 11in. (22.5cm. × 27.5cm.).*

Trees without leaves are a splendid subject for 'Thread Painting'. The drawn effect is easy to produce, by allowing the machine needle to wander across the picture.

This view of a cluster of winter trees confines the use of colour to the range of browns and greys. The background trees were filled in with random zigzags in several greys. The more clearly defined trees had to be 'drawn' more carefully with darker thread, on top of the distant trees. The meadow grass is simply blended greens, ochres and browns in a zigzag stitch, working across the picture, and widening to their fullest to make long grass in the foreground.

This subject would be a good choice for a beginner, perhaps with a simpler composition of trees and fields, because the drawing does not require exactness.

flowers by adding dots in the centre, and stalks and leaves, like the poppies in Fig. 3. These were made with a big brush full of red paint dabbed on to the background. The centres and leaves were added later. They could be stitched on to a green piece of fabric. You could add some grasses or ears of corn for a more interesting effect.

A simple landscape can be created by marking a line across the picture, to be the horizon. Below that you could paint-in grass or corn colour, and superimpose blobs of white for daisies or yellow for buttercups. A traced picture of a tree on the skyline would be sufficient to complete the scene. (See Fig. 4.)

The simplest of pictures can be most eye-catching when the 'Thread Painting' technique is used to enhance them.

Alternatively, you may wish to simplify the copying of a design on to the fabric, instead of drawing or painting freehand. Templates, torn or cut from paper or card, are useful. Arrange these on the fabric, draw around them and paint later. They are likely to make designs with neat edges, useful in geometric patterns and abstracts. You could use tracing

Fig. 3

Fig. 4

paper and dressmakers' transfer pencil to copy outlines of the design, which can then be ironed on to the background fabric. When you are tracing, be aware that images will be reversed if you turn the tracing paper over when placing it on the fabric!

With the basic outline marked out, you can then begin to paint it in with more confidence. Do not worry about making it exact. The essence of 'Thread Painting' is spontaneity.

Stage 3. Setting up the machine
a) Lower or cover up the feed teeth, according to your machine instructions for darning or free embroidery.
b) If you have a darning foot or free embroidery foot as an attachment for your machine, this can be fitted. If you prefer, the needle can be left on its own, with no foot attachment.
c) Slacken top tension just a little. This should be just sufficient to prevent any of the bobbin thread showing on top of the work.
d) Fit a fairly fine needle (70 is the finest).
e) Fill the bobbin with a neutral coloured thread (e.g. Gütermann shade 414). There is *no need* to change bobbin thread colour throughout the work.

Stage 4. Stitching the picture
SAFETY. Note that a free needle, without the protection of a sewing foot, is dangerous. Always keep fingers away from the needle as you work, and remove your foot from the accelerator when threading up.

Using your sewing machine, you can now develop and enhance the painted design with Gütermann threads.

Choose your first colour and thread up the needle. Bring up the bobbin thread.

Slip the hoop under the head of the machine.

Lower the pressure bar to engage the top tension mechanism. This will also bring the pressure foot (if being used) into position. Select required zigzag width.

Hold the thread away from you, behind the needle, and turn the wheel until the needle is in the right position on the picture.

Begin to sew slowly, while you become used to the hand-controlling of the hoop. Hold the frame at both sides to steer.

As the machine stitches, you are free to move the hoop in any direction, as fast or slowly as you wish. It does not matter if the zigzag dial is set for straight running, or wide or narrow satin stitch. You will

Following page:

English cottage garden. *Framed size 12in. × 12in. (30cm. × 30cm.); image area 7in. × 7in. (17.5cm. × 17.5cm.).*

This is an example of a smaller garden scene, being a cross between the more detailed 'Roses round the door' (page 21) and 'Abstract with flowers' (page 5).

The cottage is simple, and partly obscured by plants. The flowers are in a more controlled colour range, but mostly blobs and patches of colour, picked out by the more recognisable daisy shapes in front.

Chocolate box cottages are a favourite subject for they show how bright and lively 'Thread Painting' can be. This one features many of the techniques that I have suggested in the section on Method.

The planning was carried out first as a thumb-nail sketch on paper, and then pencilled in lightly on to the calico. Alternatively, you could use a photograph or a picture from a magazine and trace on to the calico.

In my subject there are areas of paint left unstitched, on the cottages and sky. Thatch, windows and doors have been picked out in thread to crisp up the architecture. The thatched roof lends itself to straight stitch in varying tones of straw colour for shading.

In the garden there are examples of blobs, whirls and zigzags in many colours. They are effective at a viewing distance, but can be analysed as little patches of machinery. The foreground is given the impression of nearness by the use of larger, more distinguished flower shapes, and spiky leaves.

discover that marks can be made by swirling and drawing, turning the picture round, side to side movements, and even widening and narrowing as you go along!

As a means of teaching yourself about the machine's capabilities, try out these exercises on spare calico:

a) Set zigzag dial at zero for running stitches. Begin to sew, moving the hoop away from you, giving a fairly straight line. Then start to move the hoop in a slow swirling motion, to give a spiral effect in the stitches. *NB*: not like a steering wheel, but similar to the 'panning for gold' movement.

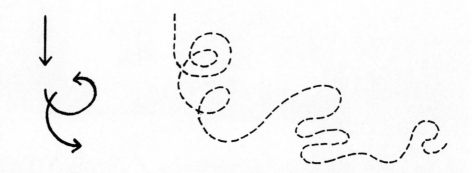

b) Set zigzag at its widest and repeat the previous exercise. You could draw some doodles on the fabric and try to go over them accurately, to gain skill.

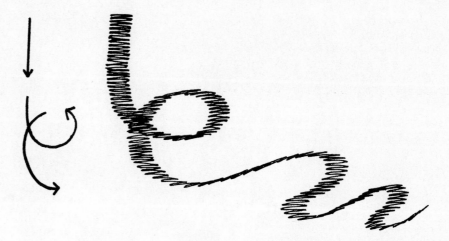

c) With zigzag at its widest setting, try moving the hoop from side to side. This should give a random 'grassy' effect. You will find this a good filling-in stitch.

d) Set zigzag at zero for running stitch, and move the hoop forward and back. Move slowly and then faster.

e) Set zigzag at half full width, and try to make little knotty patches by small swirling movements. This kind of texture is ideal for trees and clumps of flowers.

f) With stitch width at maximum, vary the closeness of threads by pushing the hoop fast or slowly away from you.

Following page:

Sunny corner. *Framed size 12in. × 12in. (30cm. × 30cm.); image area 7in. × 7in. (17.5cm. × 17.5cm.)*

In this garden scene there is very little of the house visible. Just a glimpse of window-frame makes one aware that there is a building in the picture, and helps to give an area of relief to the eye, in an overfull picture space. The flowers, this time are restricted to sunny colours of yellows, creams and golds.

This style of 'Thread Painting' is a good way to begin, because you have a small area as a controlled central point and a very wide area to explore the freedom achievable by machine.

Wheat field before harvest. *Framed size 16in. × 16in. (40cm. × 40cm.); image area 10½in. × 10½in. (26.25cm. × 26.25cm.)*

A typically English landscape, with the clear blue line of distance and rolling fields of ripened cereal. This particular one demonstrates the approach to picture-making that I have described. I worked from distance to foreground, overlapping trees and grasses. The tree texture is clearly different from the regimented zigzag of standing corn.

There is more drawing and detail in the nearest part of the picture, with ragged browns for a cluster of brambles around the old gate post, and thin wisps of straight stitch for straggling strands of grass.

The sky is left just painted, as I never try to add stitches to a smooth area. I only add texture or colour to express a particular effect.

g) With stitch width at zero, begin to move the hoop slowly away from you. As you work, turn the dial to a wider zigzag – and then narrower again. This way you can make leaf and petal shapes. (This can only be achieved if the zigzag dial on your machine allows a progressive change from one width to another. Some push-button control machines do not have the facility, but they may incorporate a 'leaf' shape in their pattern selection.)

In all kinds of free embroidery, where the feed dog has been lowered, the stitch length control will not operate. It is not necessary to set this control at all. Your speed of steering will govern the closeness of stitches.

Once you have mastered the sensation of free embroidery and have some basic control of the machine, it is time to start making a picture.

You can decide as you work which stitch width, which direction of movement, and what choice of coloured thread to use. You might even work part of the time with the picture turned away from you to achieve the right effect!

Colour in patches as you go, mingling colours, overlapping areas, and always using the machine needle like the point of a crayon.

When you work with the same coloured thread in several parts of the picture, it is easy to jump about from place to place, leaving connecting threads to be cut off later.

No finishing of ends is necessary. Just cut off threads close to the surface of your work. The under-surface will become quite messy with trailing threads from the bobbin, but there is no need to trim them up. They will always be behind the work.

Mistakes
Stitches in the wrong place can often be stitched over and hidden, without harming the quality of work. However, it may be necessary occasionally to unpick some of them with small scissors.

Sources of ideas for pictures

The medium of 'Thread Painting', like other artists' media, invites you to develop your own style and methods of working. The choice of image is entirely a matter of taste, and will be part of that individual style.

The choice of picture is a conscious decision, and is often the most daunting part of starting something new. The following ideas and suggestions are only guidelines, on which to build.

If you are beginning, it would seem to be easiest to do an abstract undefined picture, containing some of your favourite colours. Perhaps you could include some recognisable features such as flower shapes, leaves, grasses, waves or trees.

It is natural to work in this random manner, and in keeping with the speed and freedom of machining. Pictures involving features such as architecture, precision lines or geometric shapes demand more control. Any mistakes will show up only too clearly!

Landscapes and gardens are good subjects for this medium, because they feature the textures so easily produced by machine stitching. You could work directly from life, by painting straight on to the fabric, or proceed from sketches or photographs.

You might be more interested in the qualities of abstract images, using patches of colour and texture: a simple concept, such as the proportions and relationships of colours, or the play of light on threads, could be sufficient as the basis of your picture.

Another source, which might inspire a painting, is the close-up study of a scene or object, in sketches. It is possible to develop and change the subject-matter, exploring the qualities which are of greatest interest to you. The end-product might be far removed from the original.

Once you have gained the skill of movement which enables you to steer the work under the machine needle, and have discovered the potential of 'Thread Painting', you might wish to incorporate it into other craft embroidery techniques. The possibilities are considerable.

Following page:

Abstract from minerals. *Framed size 14in. × 14in. (35cm. × 35cm.); image area 8in. × 8in. (20cm. × 20cm.).*

Ideas of shapes, patterns and colours seldom spring entirely from one's own imagination. In this case, the image was inspired by my looking at rocks and minerals in a museum display. I did not do any sketching, but simply carried the colours and patterns in my memory; however if you feel you need a shape to guide you, try making a template and simply draw around it. I painted directly on to a piece of calico, with no prior planning. The resulting work hardly resembles the original source of inspiration, but it has its own spontaneous flavour, because I enlarged upon the colour theme and patterns which had excited me.

The stitch used throughout is a zigzag, mostly at its widest setting, but where the patterns radiate from a central point, the stitch size narrowed nearer the centre. The effect of crystalline forms is achieved by changing direction with little blocks of stitch, causing light to play on the texture.

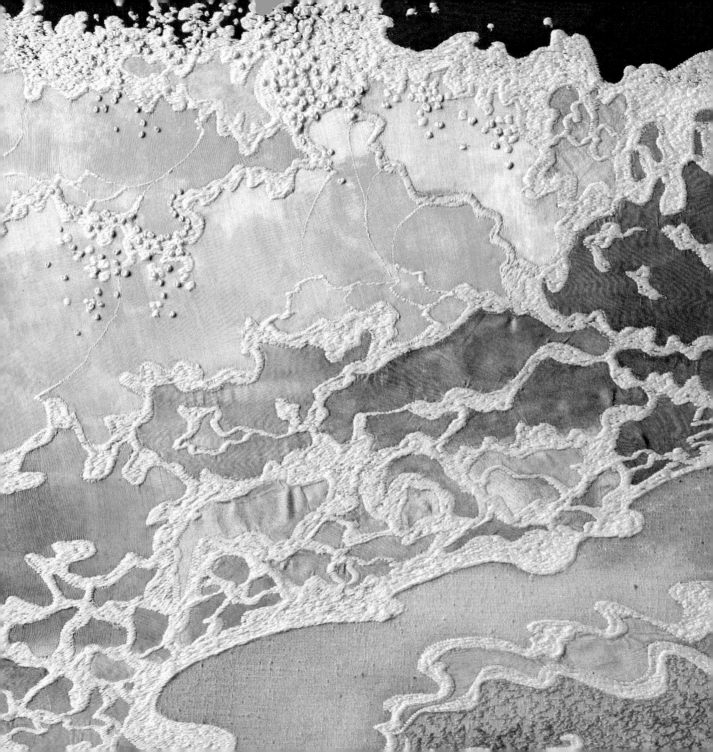

Finishing

Previous page:

Breakers. *Framed size 16in.*
(40cm. × 40cm.); image area
9½in. × 9½in.
(23.75cm. × 23.75cm.).

*Although I did not set out to do a
painting in the style of Japanese
woodcut artists, their work was in
my mind. The initial idea came from
photographs of breaking waves and
shorelines. I wanted to combine
'Thread Painting' with other forms
of embroidery and the frothy foam
and smooth glossy patches of sea
were just what I needed.*

*I divided the piece of calico into
sky at the top, and big sweeps and
curves for the shore line. I then
painted the sandy beach, before
sewing. The watery areas were
made from pieces of fine silk which I
dyed myself. The plain white silk
was dampened and dabbed and
streaked with a floppy brush loaded
with green or blue fabric dye. It was
then dried and ironed to fix the
colour.*

*These pieces were stitched down
on to the picture by machine, in a
random pattern. The joins were then
disguised with frothy 'Thread
Painting' in cream and white
thread, to give the impression of
foam.*

*I added a little machined texture
to the sand, and clusters of French
knots in stranded cottons, to give
the droplet effect of sea spray.*

While the embroidery is still in place on the frame, it remains taut. You
will notice that it buckles and distorts when removed from the frame,
because of the accumulated tension of the stitches. It will therefore need
stretching before you can display it. It is unwise to dampen the fabric
unless you are sure the paint or dye will not run.

Wrap the edges of the fabric around a piece of strong card, leaving the
picture face outwards. Lace across the back, from side to side, using a
needle and thread still on the spool.

Carry on from side to side until you have made a harp-string effect,
pulling the thread through from the spool (see Fig. 5).

Before you knot the ends, tighten the lacing as much as possible, by
flexing the card a little, so that the fabric is again stretched tight (see
Figs 6 and 7).

Repeat the procedure from top to bottom (see Fig. 8).

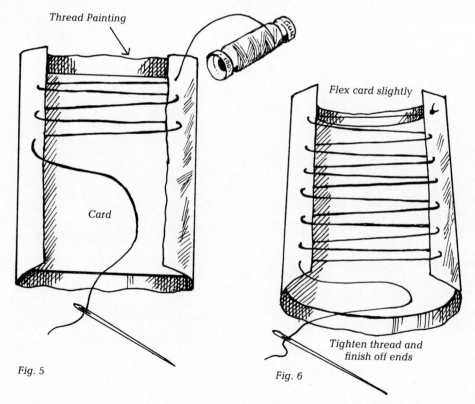

Thread Painting

Card

Flex card slightly

Tighten thread and
finish off ends

Fig. 5

Fig. 6

Framing and other applications

You may wish to frame your work. It is well worthwhile, since this enhances any picture, and it will undoubtedly surprise and please you to see the transformation.

Ready-cut mounts and frames are available. You could design your work to fit one of these standard sizes. Alternatively, a special piece could be taken to a professional framer for expert advice.

There are many other possible applications for 'Thread Painting'. It could, for example be inlaid into a sewing box lid (see page 1); a jewellery case; a photograph album. It can also be used in conjunction with other techniques such as appliqué and hand stitches.

The possibilities are as diverse as the imagination of each artist who is using this new medium. 'Thread Painting' opens up unexplored routes to creativity.

Try it, and you will see for yourself.

Flatten out again

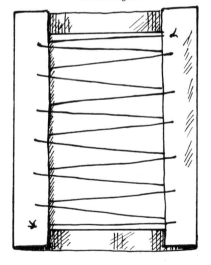

Fig. 7

Fig. 8

Acknowledgments

First published 1985 by Search Press Limited
in association with

Perivale–Gütermann Limited
Wadsworth Road, Greenford
Middlesex UB6 7JS, Great Britain

Text, reproduction, drawings, and typography,
copyright © Search Press Limited 1985. Original
'Thread Paintings' copyright © Liz Hubbard, 1985.

Reprinted 1986, 1987 (twice), 1989

'Thread Painting' is the registered trademark of Gütermann & Co. A. G., Switzerland.

Typeset by Phoenix Photosetting, Chatham.
Made and printed in Spain by A.G. Elkar, S. Coop. 48012-Bilbao   ISBN 0 85532 565 8